GEOGRAPHY OF THE WORLD

THE ANCIENT EUPHRATES

By Charnan Simon

THE CHILD'S WORLD®
CHANHASSEN, MINNESOTA

The Child's World

Published in the United States of America by The Child's World®
PO Box 326, Chanhassen, MN 55317-0326
800-599-READ
www.childsworld.com

Photo Credits: Cover/frontispiece: Nik Wheeler/Corbis.
Interior: Hakan Oge/Atlas: 4; Cuneyt Oguztuzun/Atlas: 5, 8, 9, 18; Fatih Pinar/
Atlas: 7, 12, 15, 26; Reuters/Corbis: 17; Shepard Sherbell/Corbis Saba: 13;
Ilkka Uimonen/Magnum Photos: 25; Nik Wheeler/Corbis: 20, 22, 24.

The Child's World®: Mary Berendes, Publishing Director

Editorial Directions, Inc.: E. Russell Primm, Editorial Director; Melissa McDaniel, Line
Editor; Katie Marsico, Associate Editor; Judi Shiffer, Associate Editor and Library Media
Specialist; Matthew Messbarger, Editorial Assistant; Susan Hindman, Copy Editor; Sarah
E. De Capua and Lucia Raatma, Proofreaders; Marsha Bonnoit, Peter Garnham, Terry
Johnson, Olivia Nellums, Chris Simms, Katherine Trickle, and Stephen Carl Wender,
Fact Checkers; Tim Griffin/IndexServ, Indexer; Cian Loughlin O'Day, Photo Researcher;
Linda S. Koutris, Photo Selector; XNR Productions, Inc., Cartographer

The Design Lab: Kathleen Petelinsek, Design and Page Production

Library of Congress Cataloging-in-Publication Data
Simon, Charnan.
  The ancient Euphrates / by Charnan Simon.
    p. cm. — (Geography of the world series)
  Includes index.
  ISBN 1-59296-337-4 (alk. paper)
  1. Euphrates River—Juvenile literature. I. Title. II. Series.
  DS79.89.E863S56 2004
  915.67—dc22   2004003718

Content Adviser:
Jordan Clayton,
Geography Doctoral
Candidate, University
of Colorado,
Boulder, Colorado

TABLE OF CONTENTS

CHAPTER ONE

4 The Course of the River

CHAPTER TWO

8 Plants and Animals

CHAPTER THREE

14 The Euphrates, Past and Present

CHAPTER FOUR

18 A Useful River

CHAPTER FIVE

22 People along the River

CHAPTER SIX

25 Looking to the Future

28 Glossary

29 A Euphrates River Almanac

30 The Euphrates River in the News

31 How to Learn More about the Euphrates River

32 Index

THE COURSE OF THE RIVER

The Euphrates River has a great and noble history. It is the longest river in southwestern Asia and has witnessed the birth of some of the world's oldest civilizations.

A view from the air reveals the Euphrates as it flows past Halfeti, Turkey. In size, the country of Turkey is a little bit larger than the state of Texas.

The Euphrates begins its journey in the rugged mountains of southeastern Turkey. It has two main **sources**: the Murat ("clear") and the Karasu ("muddy") rivers. These two rivers thread their way through deep, narrow gorges and across wide valleys before

The Murat River winds through Turkey's icy Diyadin Gorge. The Murat River flows 449 miles (722 kilometers).

joining to form one river, the Euphrates, near the town of Elazig.

From there, the Euphrates travels south through the stark Taurus Mountains and crosses the border into Syria. The land in Syria is mostly high, dry, and barren. People here depend on the Euphrates to water their crops in the narrow river valley.

As the Euphrates is joined by its two major **tributaries,** the Balikh and the Khabur, this valley widens. The **silt** left behind when the Euphrates floods has created rich, fertile soil. The river is surrounded by fields of cotton and grains and groves of grapefruit, oranges, and sweet lemons.

The Euphrates continues its southeasterly flow into Iraq. Now the river valley narrows once again. Dusty cliffs rise just beyond the thin strip of green. Beyond these cliffs are mile after mile of barren desert.

Past the town of Hit, the river widens. Canals and **channels** crisscross the land. These canals bring water from the Euphrates to the desert, turning it into fertile farmland. South of the town of Al-Musayyib, the Euphrates splits into two branches, the Hillah and the Hindiyah. They rejoin near the town of Samawa, about 100 miles (160 km) to the southeast.

Now the Euphrates is nearing its **mouth** at the Persian Gulf. The river slows down and splits into many channels, spreading into a vast, waterlogged marsh. Part of this marsh is really a shallow lake, called Lake Hammar. When the Euphrates flows out of Lake Hammar, it merges with the region's other great river, the Tigris. Together, the Euphrates and the Tigris rivers become known as the Shatt al Arab.

In another 120 miles (190 km), the
Shatt al Arab pours into the Persian
Gulf. The 1,700-mile (2,700-km) jour-
ney of the Euphrates River is at an end.

The Tigris and Euphrates rivers unite to form the Shatt al
Arab. This river is located in southern Iraq.

CHAPTER TWO

PLANTS AND ANIMALS

Life is harsh in the mountains of Turkey where the Euphrates begins. Winter temperatures stay well below freezing, and snow is sometimes on the ground six months of the year. Great

The Coruh River makes its way through the wintry Turkish mountains.

forests of oak, pistachio, and ash trees once covered the mountains. Today, many of these forests are gone. The Turkish government is working hard to plant new trees.

This bee-eater is one of many birds that live along the Euphrates. As their name implies, bee-eaters feed on bees, wasps, and hornets.

Farther down the mountains, wildflowers flourish in the spring. Hawks, falcons, vultures, and eagles soar overhead. Bears, deer, foxes, and rabbits roam the hillsides.

Life can also be hard on the plains and deserts where the Euphrates flows. Summer temperatures average 95° Fahrenheit (35° Celsius)—and can reach as high as 140°F (60°C). Very little rain falls in Syria and Iraq, so the Euphrates is the only source of water for most plants and animals. Camels can survive in the desert, along with some types of antelope and gazelles. Snakes, lizards, and desert rats called jerboas seek shelter under prickly camelthorn shrubs.

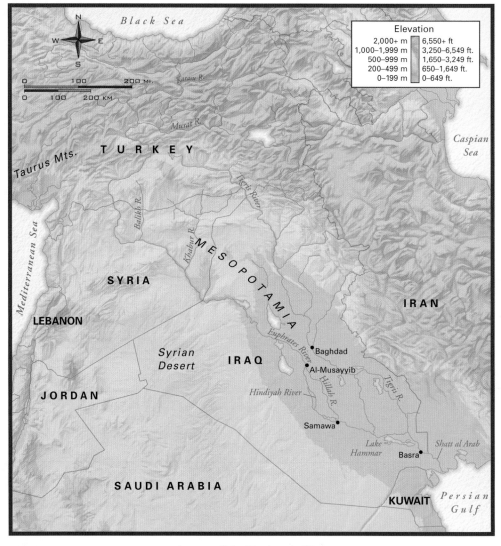

A map of the Euphrates River

Groves of willows, poplars, and eucalyptus trees flourish along the banks of the Euphrates and its canals. Small animals such as mongooses, hares, hedgehogs, and river otters seek

GIANT MARDI REED

The giant mardi reed can grow 25 feet (7.5 meters) high—as tall as a two-story building! This reed has been used to build homes and boats in the marshy regions of the Euphrates for thousands of years.

shelter in thickets of mesquite and tamarisk bushes. Larger animals such as jackals, hyenas, foxes, wolves, and gazelles come to the river to drink.

Birds love the Euphrates. Some live near the river year-round, including crows, owls, babblers, bulbuls, scrub warblers, and sand grouse. Other birds, such as pelicans, storks, and geese, follow the river as they migrate between Europe and Asia. The marshes near the river's mouth make a safe breeding ground for many of these birds.

The Iraqi marshes have long been the richest source of plant and animal life along the Euphrates. Reeds, rushes, papyrus, and cattails thrive. Frogs, toads, snakes, and turtles abound, as do carp, catfish, and spiny eels. Wild pigs roam freely, while tame water buffalo calmly munch their way through the marsh grass.

Then there are the date palm trees. Date palms have been prized in Mesopotamia since ancient times. Iraq has always been a leading grower of these tasty, nutritious fruits. As many as 18 million palm trees line the river, stretching as far as the eye can see.

Date palms flourish in Iraq and can sometimes produce fruit for more than 100 years!

An Iraqi boatman paddles through a canal along Shatt al Arab.
Canals such as this one often make travel easier, but they also destroy
the wetlands that are home to so many plants and animals.

Sadly, life along the Euphrates is not what it once was. For more

than 30 years, Iraq has been torn apart by almost constant warfare.

The entire Euphrates River valley has suffered, but perhaps no part of

it as much as the marshes of Shatt al Arab. Bombs and missiles have

wrecked cities, ports, and waterways. Dams and canals have been built

to drain the marshes. This makes it easier for soldiers and machines

to travel to and from the Persian Gulf. As much as 90 percent of the

marshes of Shatt al Arab have been destroyed in the past 30 years.

It is difficult to know just how many plant and animal **species**

have vanished along with the marsh.

CHAPTER THREE

The Euphrates, Past and Present

Mesopotamia—the fertile valley that lies between the Euphrates and the Tigris rivers—is often called "the cradle of civilization." For 7,000 years, Mesopotamia has been home to many great and powerful cultures. For all this time, people have depended on the Euphrates and Tigris rivers to bring their desert land to fruitful life.

The earliest recorded civilization along the Euphrates was Sumer. By about 5000 B.C., the farmers of Sumer were digging canals and building dams along the Euphrates to bring water to their crops. By 3000 B.C., Sumerians were living in rich, powerful cities.

The Sumerians invented many things we take for granted today. They were the first people to use plows, wheels, and calendars. More important, the Sumerians were the first humans to have a written language and number system. Carving out symbols on clay tablets, Sumerians recorded everything from crop lists to history, religion, mathematics, poetry, and astronomy. Today, scholars study surviving

These ancient ruins were once part of the city of Babylon, which was the capital of a Mesopotamian state called Babylonia.

clay tablets to learn about the rich variety of Sumerian life.

Eventually, the Sumerians began fighting among themselves. A group of people called the Akkadians conquered the area. Over thousands of years, the land of the Euphrates was conquered again and again—by the Amorites, the Babylonians, the Hittites, the Kassites, the Assyrians, the Medes, the Chaldeans, the Persians, the Greeks, and the Romans. With its rich, fertile farmland and important trade routes, Mesopotamia was a prize well worth fighting for.

Each conquering people left their mark on the lands around the Euphrates. The conquest that had the most lasting effect on modern Iraq came in A.D. 637, when warriors from the land that is now Saudi

Arabia invaded the area. The Arabs brought their language, their culture, and their religion, Islam, to Mesopotamia. Their capital, Baghdad, became the trading center of the Middle East—and the intellectual center of the Western world. Scholars came to Baghdad to study medicine, music, mathematics, poetry, religion, law, and art. Merchants sailed down the Euphrates on ships headed to China and India. They sent vast lines of camels across the deserts to Persia, Arabia, Egypt, and Syria. Today, Arabic is the official language of Iraq, and Islam is its official religion.

The lands around the Euphrates remained a prize to be fought over long after the Arabs arrived. Mongol invaders from the north repeatedly attacked Baghdad during the 13th, 14th, and 15th centuries. By the 1530s, Turkish rulers of the Ottoman Empire had taken control of the area.

The Ottoman Turks remained in power until World War I (1914–1918) ended. After the war, Great Britain took charge of Iraq. It wasn't until 1932 that Iraq finally became an independent country.

U.S. marines stationed in Iraq secure a bridge along the Euphrates. War in Iraq is destructive to both the river and the land surrounding it.

Unfortunately, independence did not bring peace. Fighting within Iraq has continued. The Iraqi king Faisal II and members of his family were killed in a revolution in 1958. Brigadier General Abd al-Karim Qasim, who led the revolution, was himself put to death in 1963. After that, President Saddam Hussein forced his country through 30 years of disastrous wars. More recently, American-led military forces overthrew Saddam Hussein. No one really knows what the future holds for the people along the Euphrates.

CHAPTER FOUR

A USEFUL RIVER

For much of its 1,700 miles (2,700 km), the Euphrates River flows through desert. In this desert, only a few inches of rain fall each year. It is blazingly hot in the summer. And yet, for thousands of years, this scorched area has been famous for its fertile farmland.

The Euphrates River is largely responsible for this fertility. Here's what happens. In early spring, snow begins melting in the Turkish

Scenic willow and polar groves dot the banks of the Euphrates in Munzur, Turkey.

mountains near the source of the Euphrates. Swollen with water from melted snow, the river flows down to the desert just as the spring rains are falling. Rainwater adds to the snowmelt from upstream, and the Euphrates overflows its banks. Rich silt, which has been carried downriver from the mountains, spills over the fields. This silt is filled with the minerals needed to grow healthy crops and helps the irrigated fields retain moisture when the hot summer temperatures return.

Since ancient times, people along the Euphrates have awaited these floods. For thousands of years, they have dug canals to channel floodwaters to their fields. They have built dams to create lakes for storing water in times of drought. Ancient people even learned to let some fields rest and be renewed each year. All these things helped ensure a bountiful crop.

Today, people in Syria and Iraq still rely on the Euphrates to **irrigate** their crops. Modern dams and canal systems help these countries produce the wheat, barley, rice, fruits, vegetables, and cotton that their people need. Dams are also used to prevent life-threatening floods and to provide much-needed electricity.

The Euphrates has never been a major shipping route. The water levels vary too much to support heavy boat traffic. In spring, the floodwaters run fast and furious. During the summer, the river becomes dangerously shallow. Smaller boats sail up and down the river, but large ocean-going ships cannot go farther upriver than the Shatt al Arab port of Basra.

CREATING NEW FARMLAND

In the past, Turkey relied more on rainfall than on the Euphrates to water its fields. But now Turkey has begun a project to build 22 dams along the upper Euphrates. Turkey hopes to use these dams to irrigate more than 30,000 square miles (80,000 sq km) of new farmland—that's just about enough farmland to feed the entire Middle East!

This dam is located along the Euphrates in Keban, Turkey, and was built during the 1960s.

Huge oil tankers cannot even make it as far as Basra. This has long been a problem for Iraq. The country has one of the world's largest supplies of oil. The most logical way to ship this oil to the rest of the world is through the Persian Gulf. But if you look at a map, you'll see that Iraq has only a tiny strip of land on the Persian Gulf. It has no port large enough to handle oil supertankers. Instead, Iraq has used a long pipeline to carry its oil 10 miles (16 km) out to sea, to a vast oil terminal. Tankers dock at this terminal to take on cargoes of oil without ever touching land.

Former president Saddam Hussein wanted more than a pipeline. He wanted greater access to the Persian Gulf. One of the reasons Iraq went to war with its neighbors, Iran and Kuwait, was to gain that access.

KALAKS

A traditional boat once used on the Euphrates was the kalak. Kalaks were log rafts that floated downriver on goatskins filled with air. Kalaks were strong, sturdy, and easy to use. When kalaks reached their destination, the goods were unloaded and the log rafts were taken apart and sold as timber. And the goatskins? They were flattened out and packed on donkeys for the return trip north. Easy!

CHAPTER FIVE

PEOPLE ALONG THE RIVER

Not many people live near the source of the Euphrates, high in the rugged mountains of Turkey. Those who do are mostly farmers. They tend hardy flocks of sheep and goats and grow just enough food for their families to eat.

A herd of sheep graze near a tributary of the Euphrates in Erzurum, Turkey. About 40 percent of the people who work in Turkey are employed as farmers.

In Syria, the Euphrates winds its way through the Syrian Desert. Irrigation has turned the land surrounding the river into rich farmland. Towns and villages dot the river valley.

Most people who live along the Euphrates are Iraqis. Almost all are followers of Islam. For many people in the Middle East, Islam is not just a religion, but a way of life. Islam guides people in what they eat and drink, how they dress, when and how they pray, and how they behave toward each other.

Until recently, most people in the Euphrates River valley lived in small villages. But in the past 30 years, many villagers moved to larger towns and cities. Iraq's rich oil reserves led to new industries and new jobs. For a while, this meant greater wealth for the Iraqi people.

Unfortunately, this has not lasted. Today, life is hard for most Iraqis. After years of war, much of their country is in ruins. Homes, schools, hospitals, and roads have been bombed. Telephones and electric lights don't work. Water faucets don't turn on, and toilets don't flush. And there isn't enough food. In a country of 20 million

Marsh Arabs make their homes on these floating islands in the Shatt al Arab wetlands. The Marsh Arab culture has existed for about 5,000 years.

to 30 million people, as many as 1 million children do not get enough to eat.

When Saddam Hussein was president of Iraq, he kept waging war against his neighbors—and against some of his own people. He used torture to stay in power.

Today, Hussein is no longer in power. But the country is still in turmoil. Only time will tell what will happen in Iraq.

CHAPTER SIX

LOOKING TO THE FUTURE

The future is uncertain for the people who live along the Euphrates River. In Iraq, years of warfare have left much of the country in ruins. It is hoped that in time Iraq's rich oil reserves may help bring wealth and stability to the Iraqi people.

Rebuilding Iraq is not the only challenge along the Euphrates. In the dry Middle East, water is even more precious

THE GARDEN OF EDEN?
In the Bible, the Euphrates is listed as one of the four rivers flowing out of the Garden of Eden. Some people believe that the Iraqi town of Qurnah, where the Euphrates and Tigris rivers join, is the site of this legendary spot where human life is said to have begun.

Workers labor at an oil refinery in Iraq.

Horses pull a boy and his wagon across the Euphrates in Birecik, Turkey. Ninety-four percent of the water that makes up the Euphrates originates in the Turkish mountains.

than oil. Turkey, Syria, and Iraq all rely on the Euphrates to water their fields, supply water in times of drought, and produce electrical power. Unless these three countries can agree to share the river's resources, there are bound to be conflicts.

There are already bitter debates. Because the Euphrates begins in Turkey, Turkey claims that it can do whatever it likes with the river. Iraq strongly disagrees. It argues that, because the Euphrates has been irrigating Iraqi lands for thousands of years, Iraq has first dibs on the river. And Syria, stuck between the two countries, claims its own rights to use the river's water.

The biggest problem is dams. Whenever dams are built, less water flows to spots farther down the river while the dam is being constructed. This can affect the timing of the river flow. After Syria built the Tabaqah Dam in 1973, Iraq claimed that 3 million Iraqi farmers could not irrigate their fields. When Turkey built the Ataturk Dam in 1990, Syria complained of losing water and electricity for more than a month. All three countries are worried that they will be cheated out of water they desperately need.

Perhaps the best solution would be for an international organization such as the United Nations to step in to help. One thing is certain: the future of the Euphrates depends on these three countries being able to work out their differences.

AN INTERNATIONAL RIVER?
One solution to the problem of who controls the Euphrates would be to classify it as an international river. This way, all the countries that use the river would have to agree to any new dams or other projects on the river.

Glossary

channels (CHAN-uhlz) Channels are the beds and streams of rivers. Sometimes, a riverbed may be dug out to make a deeper channel. Rivers also sometimes separate into two or more channels.

gorges (GORJ-ez) Gorges are deep, narrow valleys with steep sides. There is usually a river or stream at the bottom of a gorge.

irrigate (IHR-uh-gate) To irrigate is to use pipes or canals to bring water to fields. Water from the Euphrates is used to irrigate the surrounding fields.

mouth (MOUTH) The mouth of a river is the place where the river flows into the sea. The mouth of the Euphrates River is at the Persian Gulf.

silt (SILT) Silt is very fine pieces of dirt and rock carried along by river water. Silt left behind when the Euphrates floods makes the nearby fields very fertile.

sources (SORSS-ez) A river's sources are the springs, streams, or other bodies of water where it begins. The Euphrates has two main sources: the Murat and the Karasu rivers.

species (SPEE-sheez) A species is a kind of plant or animal. Many plant and animal species have vanished as the marshes of Shatt al Arab have been drained.

tributaries (TRIB-yuh-ter-eez) Tributaries are smaller streams or rivers that flow into a larger river. The Euphrates' two major tributaries are the Balikh and Khabur rivers.

A Euphrates River Almanac

Names: Shatt al-Arab (when it joins the Tigris River)

Extent
    Length: 1,700 miles (2,700 km)
    Width: Up to 1,200 feet (350 m)
    Depth: Not determined

Continent: Asia

Countries: Iraq, Syria, and Turkey

Major tributaries: Balikh and Khabur

Major cities: Al Hillah, Al-Musayyib, Basra, Hit, Qurnah, Samawa (Iraq); Abu Kamal, Dayr Az Zawr (Syria); Elazig (Turkey)

Major languages: Arabic, Kurdish, and Turkish

Parks and preserves: None

Natural resources: Oil

Native birds: Babblers, bulbuls, crows, eagles, falcons, geese, hawks, owls, pelicans, sand grouse, scrub warblers, storks, and vultures

Native fish: Carp and catfish

Native mammals: Antelopes, bears, camels, deer, foxes, gazelles, hares, hedgehogs, hyenas, jackals, jerboas, mongooses, rabbits, river otters, water buffalo, wild pigs, and wolves

Native reptiles: Lizards, snakes, and turtles

Native plants: Camelthorns, cattails, date palms, eucalyptus, giant mardi reeds, mesquite, papyrus, poplars, reeds, rushes, tamarisk, and willows

Major products: Barley, baskets, cotton, dates, fruits, rice, rope, tobacco, vegetables, and wheat

The Euphrates River in the News

5000 B.C. Sumer is the world's earliest recorded civilization. Farmers dig canals and build dams to use the water from the Euphrates.

3000 B.C. The Sumerian civilization becomes wealthy and powerful.

A.D. 637 Warriors from Saudi Arabia invade the land of the Euphrates, bringing Arabic and Islam with them.

1200s–1400s Mongol invaders repeatedly attack Baghdad.

1530 Turkish rulers of the Ottoman Empire take control of Baghdad.

1918 Great Britain takes charge of Iraq.

1932 Iraq becomes an independent country.

1973 Syria builds the Tabaqah Dam.

1990 Turkey builds the Ataturk Dam.

2003 American-led military forces overthrow Iraqi leader Saddam Hussein.

How to Learn More about the Euphrates River

At the Library

Foster, Leila Merrell. *Iraq*. Danbury, Conn.: Children's Press, 1998.

Orr, Tamra. *Turkey*. Danbury, Conn.: Children's Press, 2003.

Whitcraft, Melissa. *The Tigris and Euphrates Rivers*. Danbury, Conn.: Franklin Watts, 1999.

Wilkinson, Philip. *Islam*. New York: DK Publishing, 2002.

On the Web

VISIT OUR HOME PAGE FOR LOTS OF LINKS ABOUT THE EUPHRATES RIVER:

http://www.childsworld.com/links.html

Note to Parents, Teachers, and Librarians: We routinely verify our Web links to make sure they're safe, active sites—so encourage your readers to check them out!

Places to Visit or Contact

EMBASSY OF IRAQ

1801 P Street NW

Washington DC 20036

EMBASSY OF THE REPUBLIC OF TURKEY

2525 Massachusetts Avenue NW

Washington, DC 20008

EMBASSY OF SYRIA

2215 Wyoming Avenue NW

Washington, DC 20008

Index

Akkadians, 15
Al-Musayyib, Iraq, 6
animal life, 9, 10, 11–12, 13
Arabic language, 16
Arabs, 16
Ataturk Dam, 27

Baghdad, Iraq, 16
Balikh River, 5
Basra, Iraq, 20, 21
birds, 9, 11

canals, 6, 13, 14
channels, 6
climate, 8, 9, 18

dams, 13, 14, 20, 27
date palms, 12
deserts, 6, 9, 10, 23

electricity, 20

Faisal II (king), 17
farming, 6, 14, 15, 18, 19–20,
    22, 27
fish, 11
flooding, 5, 19, 20
forests, 9

Garden of Eden, 25
giant mardi reed, 11
Great Britain, 17

Hanging Gardens of Babylon, 16
Hillah River, 6
Hindiyah River, 6
Hit, Iraq, 6
Hussein, Saddam, 17, 21, 24

Iran, 21
Iraq, 6, 9, 11, 12, 13, 15, 16, 17,
    19, 21, 23, 24, 25, 26–27
irrigation, 19, 20, 23, 27
Islamic religion, 16, 23

kalaks, 21
Karasu River, 5
Khabur River, 5
Kuwait, 21

Lake Hammar, 6

Marsh Arabs, 24
marshes, 6, 11, 24
Mesopotamia, 7, 12, 14, 15, 16
Mongols, 16
mouth, 6, 7
Murat River, 5

Nebuchadnezzar II (king), 16
oil, 25
Ottoman Empire, 16–17

people, 14–17, 22, 23–24
Persian Gulf, 6, 7, 21
plant life, 9, 10, 11, 12, 13

Qasim, Abd al-Karim, 17
Qurnah, Iraq, 25

Samawa, Iraq, 6
Shatt al Arab, 6–7, 13, 20, 24
shipping, 20
silt, 5, 19
sources, 4–5, 19
Sumerians, 14–15, 24
Syria, 5, 9, 16, 19, 23, 26, 27

Tabaqah Dam, 27
Taurus Mountains, 5
Tigris River, 6, 7
transportation, 20–21
trees, 9, 11, 12
tributaries, 5
Turkey, 4, 7, 8–9, 20, 22, 26, 27

war, 13, 17, 21, 23, 24, 25

About the Author

Charnan Simon has a BA in English literature from Carleton College and an MA in English literature from the University of Chicago. She has been at editor at both *Cricket* and *Click* magazines and has written more than 50 books for young readers. Ms. Simon lives in Madison, Wisconsin, with her husband Tom, their daughters, Ariel and Hana, Sam the dog, and Lily and Luna the cats.

9/06,2